Materials

Plastic

Cassie Mayer

Heinemann
LIBRARY

www.heinemann.co.uk/library
Visit our website to find out more information about Heinemann Library books.

To order:
☎ Phone 44 (0) 1865 888066
▤ Send a fax to 44 (0) 1865 314091
▭ Visit the Heinemann Bookshop at www.heinemann.co.uk/library to browse our
catalogue and order online.

First published in Great Britain by Heinemann Library,
Halley Court, Jordan Hill, Oxford OX2 8EJ, part of Pearson
Education. Heinemann is a registered trademark of Pearson
Education Ltd.

Editorial: Diyan Leake
Design: Joanna Hinton-Malivoire
Picture research: Tracy Cummins and Heather Mauldin
Production: Duncan Gilbert

Originated by Chroma Graphics (Overseas) Pte Ltd
Printed and bound in China by South China Printing Co. Ltd

ISBN 978 0 431 19258 1
12 11 10 09 08
10 9 8 7 6 5 4 3 2 1

British Library Cataloguing in Publication Data follows:
Mayer, Cassie
  Plastic. - (Materials)
  1. Plastics - Juvenile literature
  I. Title
  620.1'923

Acknowledgments
The author and publisher are grateful to the following
for permission to reproduce copyright material: © Corbis
pp. **4** (Lowell Georgia), **12** (SYGM/Vo Trung Dunga), **15**
(David Pollack), **20**, **22** bottom (Schlegelmilch); © Getty
Images pp. **5** (Time Line Pictures/Sergio Dorantes), **9**
(George Diebold), **11**, **23** top (Darren McCollester);
© Heinemann Raintree pp. **7**, **14**, **16**, **17**, **18**, **19**, **21**,
22 middle, **22** top, **23** bottom (David Rigg); © Jupiter
Images pp. **10**, **23** middle (Creatas Images); © The
New York Times p. **13** (Redux/Hans Rudolf Oeser);
© Shutterstock pp. **6** (Prism_68), **8** (TIMURA).

Cover image used with permission of © Corbis (Perry
Mastrovito). Back cover image used with permission of
© Shutterstock (Prism_68).
Every effort has been made to contact copyright holders of
any material reproduced in this book. Any omissions will
be rectified in subsequent printings if notice is given to the
publisher.

Contents

What is plastic?

Plastic is a material.

It is made from oil.

It is made by people.

Plastic can be strong.

Plastic can be light.

Plastic can be stiff.

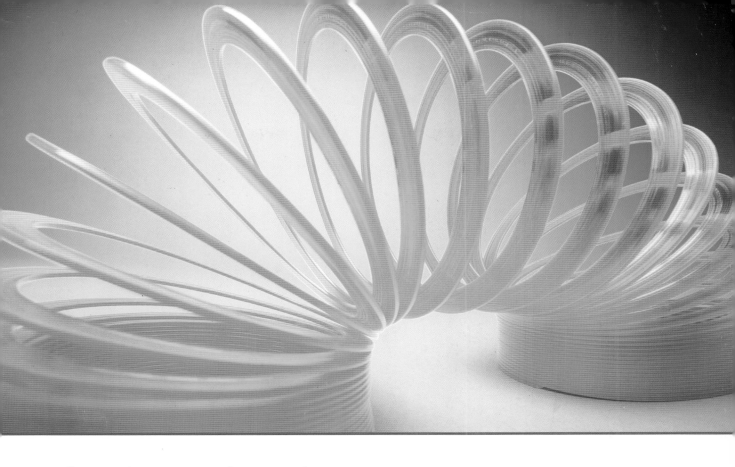

Plastic can bend.

What happens when plastic is heated?

Plastic can be heated.

Plastic becomes a liquid when
it is heated.

When plastic is heated, it can be
made into a new shape.

After it is heated, plastic can cool down and become hard again.

Recycling plastic

Plastic can be recycled.

It can be used to make new plastic things.

Plastic can be used to make playground equipment.

Plastic can be used to make bottles and boxes.

How do people use plastic?

Plastic can be used to make drinking bottles.

Plastic can be used to make toys.

Plastic can be used to make
racing cars.

Plastic can be used to make lots
of things.

Things made of plastic

◀ containers

▼ racing car

◀ toy

Picture glossary

 **liquid** something that flows and takes the shape of the container it is in. Water is a liquid.

 **melt** change from a solid to a liquid. Plastic is a material that melts when it is heated.

 **recycle** take old things to make them into new things

Content vocabulary for teachers

material something that can be used to make things

Index

Notes for parents and teachers

Before reading   Put items made of materials such as wood, plastic, metal, and rubber in a closed bag. Challenge the children to feel in the bag and, without looking, identify the object made of plastic. What did it feel like? Was it cold to touch? Was it heavy or light? Talk about the properties of plastic. Ask the children what things they own made of plastic.

After reading

• Put a variety of different toys, including plastic toys, on a tray. Give the children two minutes to memorize all the plastic toys. Then cover the tray with a cloth and challenge them to remember all the plastic toys.

• Talk about recycling plastic. Do they think it is a good idea? Make a class poster based on "Reduce, Re-use, Recycle".

• Plastic comes in a wide range of colours. Encourage children to bring in small items made of plastic. Can they find things of different colours?